HOW TO FLIP HOUSES FOR BEGINNERS

Mastering Real Estate Profits from MLS Mastery to Design Brilliance, Learn the Secrets of Rapid Returns and Tax-Saving Strategies

Jerry R. Schaefer

i

OTHER BOOKS BY SAME AUTHOR

1. HOW TO INVEST FOR TEENAGERS
2. HOW TO INVEST $10,000 INTO FINANCIAL FREEDOM
3. HOW TO BUDGET AND SAVE MONEY FOR BEGINNERS
4. THE PATH TO LONG-TERM INVESTMENT
5. FINANCIAL INDEPENDENCE WITH 70% SAVING
6. ONE YEAR TO FINANCIAL FREEDOM
7. INVESTING STRATEGIES FOR ANY BUDGET
8. FROM YOUR FIRST $100K
9. HOW TO INVEST FOR BEGINNERS

TABLE OF CONTENTS

Introduction

Welcome to the thrilling world of house flipping, where strategic decisions, bold moves, and creative designs pave the way to financial prosperity. In this journey, we'll embark on an exciting exploration of the art and science of turning distressed properties into lucrative assets.

Overview of House Flipping

House flipping, at its core, is the process of purchasing a property, renovating or upgrading it, and then selling it for a profit. However, it's much more than a mere renovation project; it's a strategic dance with the real estate market, a game of numbers, and an opportunity to unleash your creativity in design.

Beyond the do-it-yourself home improvement shows, real-life house flipping involves understanding market trends, evaluating deals, and making decisions that can significantly impact your bottom line. It's a journey filled with challenges, triumphs, and the potential for substantial financial gains.

Before we delve into the intricacies of house flipping, let's acknowledge the fundamental principle that fuels success in real estate—taking action. While knowledge is crucial, the power to turn dreams into reality lies in decisive steps forward. In this book, we'll guide you through actionable steps, sharing insights from experienced flippers, and providing a roadmap to navigate the complexities of the real estate market.

Are you intrigued by the prospect of transforming neglected properties into lucrative investments? Perhaps you've watched television shows featuring dramatic transformations, but now you're ready to step into the realm of real-world house flipping. This book is your compass, designed to simplify the process, break down key concepts, and empower you to take the first steps toward your own success in the world of house flipping.

Whether you're a novice investor or someone with prior real estate experience looking to diversify your portfolio, this book is crafted to offer practical advice in simple language. We believe that everyone can grasp the principles of house flipping, and by the end of this journey, you'll have the tools, knowledge, and confidence to embark on your own flipping adventure.

Get ready to explore the nuts and bolts of house flipping, from finding the right properties on the market to mastering the art of creative design that not only adds aesthetic appeal but also boosts your return on investment. We'll guide you through the challenges and solutions encountered during the renovation process, share insights into competitive pricing for a quick sale, and unravel the mysteries of financing and taxes in the realm of real estate.

So, buckle up and prepare to uncover the secrets, strategies, and success stories that will shape your understanding of house flipping. This book is more than a guide; it's your companion on a journey to financial growth, one flip at a time.

The Power of Taking Action

In the vast landscape of possibilities, dreams remain dormant until awakened by the one force that breathes life into aspirations—the power of taking action. It is this dynamic force that propels individuals from the realm of contemplation into the arena of tangible achievements. Nowhere is this transformative power more evident than in the world of house flipping, where decisive steps forward distinguish dreamers from achievers.

Taking action is not merely a step; it is a mindset, an unwavering commitment to convert vision into reality. In the context of house flipping, it is the catalyst that turns dilapidated structures into profitable assets, and it often marks the defining line between success and stagnation.

The journey of a successful house flipper begins with the audacity to act on a vision. Imagine spotting a neglected property, visualizing its potential, and then taking the leap to acquire it. This bold move sets the stage for a series of calculated decisions and transformative efforts that culminate in a profitable outcome. The real power lies not just in the acquisition but in the courage to initiate the process.

Procrastination, fueled by fear or uncertainty, can stifle the most promising endeavors. House flipping, like any entrepreneurial venture, requires risk-taking and a willingness to embrace the unknown. The power of taking action is not about making impulsive decisions; rather, it's about recognizing opportunities, conducting due diligence, and then boldly stepping forward when the time is right.

In the realm of house flipping, those who harness the power of taking action are often met with a domino effect of positive outcomes. The act of acquiring a property initiates a chain reaction, leading to strategic renovations, market-savvy decisions, and ultimately, a profitable sale. It is a journey where each action begets another, propelling the flipper forward with momentum.

Success in house flipping is not reserved for the seasoned investor alone. The power of taking action levels the playing field, inviting novices to enter the arena and learn by doing. It encourages individuals to overcome analysis paralysis, embrace challenges as opportunities for growth, and continually refine their approach through hands-on experience.

This power extends beyond the initial acquisition; it permeates every stage of the flipping process. From formulating a renovation strategy to pricing the property competitively, each decision is an action that shapes the outcome. Even in the face of setbacks or unforeseen challenges, the power of taking action empowers flippers to adapt, learn, and navigate the complexities of real estate.

In conclusion, the power of taking action is the beating heart of house flipping success. It transforms dreams into reality, propels individuals from contemplation to achievement, and cultivates a mindset that thrives on calculated risk and resilience. Aspiring flippers, heed this call to action, for it is the force that will set your journey ablaze and lead you towards the realization of your real estate aspirations.

Finding Gold on the MLS

In the dynamic world of real estate investing, the Multiple Listing Service (MLS) stands as a treasure trove, holding the keys to potential gold mines for savvy investors. This chapter is your compass to navigating the real estate market through the MLS, providing insights into strategies that can unearth lucrative opportunities and set you on the path to successful house flipping.

Navigating the Real Estate Market

At the heart of the real estate market lies the MLS, a comprehensive database of properties listed for sale. While it might seem like a simple online platform, the MLS is a powerful tool that grants access to a vast array of properties, including those not visible to the general public. For house flippers, it is a gateway to potential investments, a realm where hidden gems await discovery.

To navigate the real estate market effectively, understanding the intricacies of the MLS is paramount. Real estate professionals, such as agents and brokers, contribute to the MLS, ensuring that it remains a centralized hub of property information. As an investor, forging relationships with these professionals can provide you with valuable insights, early access to listings, and a competitive edge in the market.

The MLS is not just a static repository of listings; it's a dynamic landscape that demands a strategic approach. Savvy investors employ filters and search criteria to sift through the myriad of listings and identify properties aligning with their investment goals. From location preferences to budget constraints, refining your search on the MLS enables you to pinpoint potential gold mines amidst the sea of available properties.

Strategies for success on the MLS extend beyond conventional searches. Investors often employ advanced techniques, such as setting up automated alerts for specific criteria or leveraging data analytics tools to identify emerging trends. Staying ahead in the real estate market requires a proactive stance, and the MLS offers a platform for investors to be at the forefront of available opportunities.

In addition to the technical aspects of navigating the MLS, building strong relationships with real estate professionals can be a game-changer. Establishing rapport with agents who specialize in your target market can provide you with valuable off-market opportunities—properties not yet listed on the MLS. This off-market access is akin to having a first pick in a hidden treasure chest, giving you a head start in a competitive market.

Successful navigation of the real estate market also involves adapting to its ever-evolving nature. Market conditions, property values, and buyer preferences are dynamic factors that influence investment decisions. Regularly monitoring the MLS and staying informed about market trends empower you to make well-informed decisions that align with the current landscape.

In conclusion, the journey to finding gold on the MLS is a multifaceted one, combining technical prowess with strategic networking. Navigating the real estate market is not a passive endeavor; it requires an active engagement with the MLS, a keen understanding of search strategies, and the cultivation of relationships with key players in the industry. As you embark on your quest for real estate success, let the MLS be your guiding star, illuminating the path to profitable investments and unlocking the potential for house flipping triumphs.

Strategies for Successful MLS Purchases

In the intricate dance of real estate investment, mastering the art of successful Multiple Listing Service (MLS) purchases is paramount. This chapter unveils strategic approaches that can elevate your game, ensuring that you not only identify promising properties but also secure them in a competitive market, setting the stage for prosperous house flipping ventures.

Understanding the MLS Landscape

To harness the full potential of the MLS, investors must first gain a nuanced understanding of its landscape. The MLS is a dynamic platform where properties are listed for sale, but not all listings are created equal. Recognizing that the MLS is a reflection of the broader real estate market allows investors to tailor their strategies to the ever-changing conditions of the field.

Early Engagement with Real Estate Professionals

One key strategy for successful MLS purchases involves establishing early engagement with real estate professionals. Agents and brokers are often the gatekeepers of valuable information, and forming strong relationships with them can provide you with insights into off-market opportunities and exclusive access to pre-listed properties. By actively networking with these professionals, you position yourself to receive notifications about potential deals before they hit the broader market.

Refining Search Criteria for Precision

A crucial aspect of successful MLS purchases lies in the ability to refine search criteria with precision. The MLS offers a myriad of filters and options that allow investors to tailor their searches to specific parameters. From location and property type to budget constraints and desired features, leveraging these filters narrows down the field, enabling you to focus on properties that align with your investment goals.

Automation and Alerts: A Proactive Approach

In the fast-paced world of real estate, being proactive is key. Savvy investors use automation tools and set up alerts within the MLS to receive real-time notifications for new listings that match their criteria. This proactive approach ensures that you stay ahead of the competition, swiftly identifying opportunities as soon as they become available. Automation tools not only save time but also enhance your ability to act swiftly in a competitive market.

Data Analytics for Informed Decision-Making

Embracing data analytics is another strategy that can significantly enhance your chances of successful MLS purchases. Investors can leverage analytical tools to assess market trends, property values, and potential growth areas. By incorporating data-driven insights into your decision-making process, you can make informed choices that align with the current dynamics of the real estate market.

Strategic Offers and Negotiation

Successfully securing a property from the MLS involves more than just identifying opportunities; it requires strategic offers and negotiation skills. Understanding the market value of a property, analyzing comparable sales data, and crafting compelling offers are essential components of this strategy. A nuanced negotiation approach, backed by market knowledge, increases the likelihood of your offer being accepted in a competitive marketplace.

Adapting to Market Conditions

Flexibility and adaptability are virtues in the realm of real estate. Successful MLS purchases require investors to adapt their strategies based on market conditions. Whether it's adjusting search criteria, fine-tuning negotiation tactics, or reevaluating investment goals, the ability to adapt ensures that you remain agile and resilient in the face of an ever-evolving real estate landscape.

Building a Robust Portfolio Through MLS Mastery

In conclusion, mastery of the MLS is not just about accessing a database; it's about implementing strategic approaches that position you for success. Early engagement with real estate professionals, precise search criteria, proactive automation, data analytics, and strategic negotiation are the cornerstones of successful MLS purchases. As you navigate the complex terrain of real estate investment, let these strategies be your compass, guiding you towards a portfolio enriched with lucrative properties and ensuring your place among successful house flippers.

The 70% Rule: Your Winning Formula for Real Estate Success

In the intricate world of real estate investing, where precision and strategy reign supreme, the 70% Rule stands as a beacon of guidance for savvy investors seeking to secure profitable deals. This chapter unveils the essence of the 70% Rule, a winning formula that has become a cornerstone in the arsenal of successful house flippers.

Understanding the 70% Rule: Decoding the Formula

At its core, the 70% Rule is a formula designed to help investors make informed decisions about the maximum purchase price for a property. The rule asserts that an investor should not pay more than 70% of the after-repair value (ARV) of a property, minus the estimated repair costs. This seemingly simple equation becomes a powerful tool when wielded with precision, offering a strategic approach to evaluating potential investments.

Let's break down the components of the 70% Rule:

- After-Repair Value (ARV): This is the estimated future value of the property after renovations and improvements are made. Accurately assessing the ARV is crucial, as it forms the basis for determining the upper limit on the purchase price.

- Repair Costs: These are the estimated expenses associated with renovating and improving the property to reach its optimal condition. A detailed understanding of repair costs is essential for a realistic evaluation of the property's overall investment potential.

- Maximum Purchase Price: Calculated by taking 70% of the ARV and subtracting the estimated repair costs, this figure represents the highest amount an investor should be willing to pay for the property.

Why the 70% Rule Matters: Mitigating Risks and Maximizing Returns

The 70% Rule serves as a risk mitigation strategy and a mechanism to ensure that investors enter deals with a sufficient margin of safety. By adhering to this rule, investors guard against overpaying for a property, leaving room for unforeseen challenges or unexpected expenses that may arise during the renovation process.

21

One of the key benefits of the 70% Rule is its role in maximizing returns. By setting a purchase price that aligns with the 70% threshold, investors create a buffer that allows for both profitable resale and room for unexpected costs. This strategic approach positions investors to not only recover their investment but also generate a substantial profit upon selling the renovated property.

Practical Application of the 70% Rule

Consider a hypothetical scenario: A property has an estimated ARV of $200,000, and the repair costs are projected to be $30,000. Applying the 70% Rule, the maximum purchase price would be calculated as follows:

$Maximum\ Purchase\ Pric = 70\% \times ARV - Repair\ Costs$

$Maximum\ Purchase\ Price$

$= 0.7 \times \$200,000 - \$30,000$

$= \$140,000 - \$30,000$

$= \$110,000$

In this case, the investor should not pay more than $110,000 for the property to align with the 70% Rule.

Realizing the Potential: Making Informed Investment Decisions

The 70% Rule is not a rigid dictate but rather a guiding principle that empowers investors to make informed decisions. It provides a systematic approach to evaluating deals, ensuring that the purchase price is in harmony with the property's potential for profitable resale.

In conclusion, the 70% Rule is not merely a mathematical formula; it is a winning strategy that empowers investors to navigate the complexities of real estate with confidence. By understanding and applying this rule, investors can mitigate risks, maximize returns, and lay the foundation for successful ventures in the competitive arena of house flipping. As you embark on your real estate journey, let the 70% Rule be your compass, guiding you towards well-calculated investments and the realization of your financial aspirations.

Evaluating Deals Like a Pro

In the dynamic realm of real estate investment, the ability to evaluate deals with precision is a skill that separates novices from seasoned professionals. This chapter unravels the art and science of evaluating deals like a pro, shedding light on the key considerations, methodologies, and strategic approaches that pave the way for successful real estate ventures.

The Intersection of Art and Science

Evaluating real estate deals is a nuanced process that harmonizes both art and science. The art lies in the ability to envision a property's potential, foresee market trends, and conceptualize the final product after renovations. This creative aspect involves tapping into intuition, experience, and a keen eye for design—traits that seasoned investors cultivate over time.

On the other hand, the science of deal evaluation involves rigorous analysis, data-driven decision-making, and a systematic approach to assessing the financial viability of a property. It encompasses crunching numbers, conducting market research, and utilizing various financial metrics to ensure that an investment aligns with predetermined criteria.

Key Considerations in Deal Evaluation

- After-Repair Value (ARV): Central to deal evaluation is the determination of a property's ARV—the estimated value after renovations. Accurate ARV assessment is foundational, as it influences the entire investment strategy and sets the upper limit for the purchase price.

- Repair Costs: A meticulous understanding of repair costs is crucial. This involves itemizing the necessary renovations, obtaining accurate cost estimates from contractors, and factoring in potential contingencies. Precision in estimating repair costs safeguards against budget overruns.

- Market Conditions: Successful deal evaluation requires a keen awareness of current market conditions. Is the local real estate market on an upward trend? Are there emerging neighborhoods with growth potential? Understanding these dynamics informs investment decisions and influences the exit strategy.

- Location Analysis: The adage "location, location, location" holds true in real estate. Evaluating the neighborhood's desirability, proximity to amenities, and potential for appreciation is pivotal. A property in a sought-after location often commands a higher resale value.

- Comparable Sales (Comps): Analyzing comparable sales in the area provides a benchmark for assessing a property's value. Examining recent sales of similar properties aids in gauging market value and determining an appropriate asking price.

Strategic Approaches to Deal Evaluation

- The 1% Rule: A rule of thumb in real estate is the 1% Rule, which suggests that the monthly rental income should ideally be at least 1% of the property's purchase price. While not a rigid guideline, it offers a quick assessment of a property's potential cash flow.

- Cap Rate: The Capitalization Rate, or Cap Rate, is a financial metric that evaluates the return on an investment property. Calculated by dividing the property's net operating income by its current market value, the Cap Rate provides insights into the property's profitability.

- Cash-on-Cash Return: This metric assesses the return on the actual cash invested in the property. It considers factors such as financing, operating income, and expenses to provide a more nuanced understanding of the return on investment.

- Risk Mitigation Strategies: Evaluating deals like a pro involves considering potential risks and implementing mitigation strategies. Assessing the neighborhood's stability, conducting thorough property inspections, and having contingency plans for unexpected challenges are integral parts of the evaluation process.

The Decision-Making Nexus

At the nexus of art and science, the seasoned investor makes informed decisions based on a holistic evaluation of the deal. Evaluating deals like a pro goes beyond crunching numbers; it requires a comprehensive understanding of market dynamics, property potential, and the investor's overarching financial goals.

A Case Study in Deal Evaluation

Consider a hypothetical scenario: A property has an estimated ARV of $250,000, repair costs are projected at $40,000, and the market dictates a competitive purchase price. Applying the 70% Rule—ensuring the purchase price does not exceed 70% of the ARV minus repair costs—the maximum purchase price is calculated:

Maximum Purchase Price = 70% ×ARV-Repair Costs

Maximum Purchase Price=70%×ARV−Repair Costs

Maximum Purchase Price=0.7×$250,000-$40,000 = $175,000-$40,000=$135,000

Maximum Purchase Price =0.7×$250,000-$40,000

=$175,000-$40,000 =$135,000

This calculated figure becomes the threshold for negotiating and securing the property within a strategically viable range.

In conclusion, evaluating deals like a pro demands a synthesis of intuition, analysis, and strategic thinking. Successful investors navigate the complex landscape of real estate with a discerning eye, leveraging both the art and science of deal evaluation. By incorporating key considerations, strategic approaches, and decision-making metrics, aspiring investors can embark on a journey towards mastering the art of evaluating deals—a skill that propels them toward profitable ventures in the ever-evolving world of real estate.

Unleashing Creative Design

In the dynamic arena of real estate, where aesthetics meet functionality, the strategic deployment of creative design emerges as a powerful tool for enhancing property value and investor success. This chapter delves into the transformative influence of open spaces, unraveling the art and impact of integrating innovative design concepts into real estate ventures.

The Evolution of Open Spaces: Beyond Aesthetics

Open spaces have transcended their role as mere aesthetic enhancements; they have become integral components of modern design that significantly influence the perceived value and functionality of a property. As the demand for contemporary and versatile living spaces rises, the judicious use of open layouts has become a hallmark of forward-thinking real estate design.

Maximizing Natural Light and Airflow

One of the key benefits of incorporating open spaces is the maximization of natural light and airflow. By removing unnecessary walls and barriers, sunlight permeates freely throughout the space, creating an ambiance that is not only visually appealing but also contributes to energy efficiency. Ample airflow enhances ventilation, creating a refreshing atmosphere that aligns with the preferences of today's discerning homeowners.

The Illusion of Spaciousness

Open spaces wield a transformative power by creating the illusion of spaciousness. This is particularly impactful in smaller properties, where the removal of walls and partitions can visually expand the available square footage. The perception of a larger living area not only enhances the overall appeal of the property but also adds to its market desirability.

Facilitating Social Connectivity

In an era where the concept of home as a sanctuary is evolving, open spaces facilitate social connectivity. Open floor plans seamlessly integrate living, dining, and kitchen areas, fostering an environment conducive to interaction and shared experiences. This design approach resonates with contemporary lifestyles, where families and friends seek fluid spaces that accommodate both individual pursuits and communal activities.

Adaptable and Multi-Functional Design

Open spaces embody adaptability and multi-functional design, responding to the diverse needs of inhabitants. The removal of walls allows for flexible configurations, enabling residents to customize their living spaces according to changing preferences or specific occasions. This adaptability not only enhances the overall utility of the property but also caters to the dynamic nature of modern living.

The Impact on Property Value

The integration of open spaces goes beyond aesthetic appeal; it has a tangible impact on property value. Homes featuring open layouts are often perceived as more desirable in the real estate market, attracting a broader range of potential buyers. The increased demand for properties with open designs translates into heightened market competitiveness and, consequently, enhanced resale value.

Innovative Design Concepts: Cable Ropes and Accent Walls

Within the realm of creative design, innovative concepts such as cable ropes and accent walls play a pivotal role in elevating the aesthetic appeal of open spaces. Cable ropes, popular in construction and modern design, add a contemporary touch to staircases, contributing to a sleek and minimalist aesthetic. Accent walls, inspired by trends seen on design platforms like HGTV, introduce a focal point within open areas, creating visual interest and personalization.

Navigating Challenges in Open Design

While the advantages of open spaces are abundant, navigating potential challenges is essential for successful implementation. Structural considerations, electrical rewiring, and addressing unexpected issues that arise when walls are removed require a thorough understanding of the property and experienced project management.

In conclusion, unleashing creative design, particularly through the incorporation of open spaces, transcends conventional notions of property enhancement. The strategic use of open layouts, maximization of natural elements, and integration of innovative design concepts contribute to a property's appeal, functionality, and market value. As real estate investors embrace the transformative power of open spaces, they embark on a journey where art, functionality, and market dynamics converge, creating homes that resonate with the evolving preferences of the modern homeowner.

Trendy Design Elements for Maximum ROI

In the ever-evolving landscape of real estate, staying attuned to the latest design trends is not merely a matter of aesthetics—it's a strategic imperative for investors seeking maximum return on investment (ROI). This chapter explores trendy design elements that transcend fleeting fads, providing a comprehensive guide to elevating your real estate ventures and ensuring they stand out in a competitive market.

Contemporary Minimalism: The Timeless Allure

Embracing the ethos of contemporary minimalism is a design choice that transcends trends and endures through time. Clean lines, uncluttered spaces, and a neutral color palette define this aesthetic, creating an environment that exudes sophistication and broad market appeal. Minimalist interiors not only offer a timeless allure but also provide a versatile canvas for prospective homeowners to infuse their personal style.

Open Shelving and Smart Storage Solutions

In the realm of kitchen and bathroom design, open shelving has emerged as a trend that seamlessly combines functionality with visual appeal. Open shelves create an airy and modern ambiance, while also encouraging a more organized approach to storage. Smart storage solutions, such as pull-out cabinets and multifunctional furniture, further enhance the usability of spaces, catering to the practical needs of modern living.

Bold Backsplashes and Statement Tiles

Elevate the visual impact of kitchens and bathrooms by incorporating bold backsplashes and statement tiles. Whether it's a vibrant mosaic, geometric pattern, or textured surface, these design elements infuse personality into spaces that are often considered focal points in a home. Bold choices in backsplashes and tiles not only capture attention but also contribute to a memorable and distinctive overall design.

Natural Elements: Biophilic Design

Incorporating natural elements into interior design—a concept known as biophilic design—is a trend that transcends style preferences. Biophilic design integrates nature-inspired elements such as natural light, indoor plants, and organic textures. Beyond the aesthetic appeal, this design approach has been linked to enhanced well-being and improved mental health, making it a sought-after feature for homeowners.

Smart Home Technology Integration

The intersection of design and technology has given rise to the integration of smart home features. From automated lighting and thermostats to security systems and voice-activated controls, incorporating smart technology enhances the property's appeal, functionality, and efficiency. Prospective buyers increasingly seek homes equipped with these modern conveniences, positioning properties with smart home integration for a competitive edge in the market.

Luxurious Finishes: Matte Black and Gold Accents

Elevate the perception of luxury within a property by incorporating sophisticated finishes. Matte black and gold accents, in particular, have become synonymous with contemporary elegance. From faucets and cabinet hardware to light fixtures and door handles, these finishes add a touch of opulence, creating a high-end ambiance that resonates with discerning buyers.

Flexible Workspaces: Adapting to Remote Lifestyles

The shift towards remote work has underscored the importance of flexible and functional home office spaces. Designating an area that seamlessly integrates into the overall aesthetic of a home while catering to the practical needs of remote work is a trend that aligns with the evolving lifestyles of potential buyers. Versatile spaces that can serve as both work and relaxation zones enhance a property's market desirability.

In the realm of real estate investment, leveraging trendy design elements is not merely a stylistic choice—it's a strategic blueprint for success. By embracing contemporary minimalism, integrating smart technology, and incorporating luxurious finishes, investors can elevate their properties, ensuring they align with the preferences of the modern homeowner. The synergy of these design elements goes beyond aesthetics, creating homes that not only captivate buyers but also command a premium in the competitive real estate market. As you embark on your journey to maximize ROI, let innovative design be your guiding principle, shaping properties that transcend trends and leave a lasting impression on the discerning market.

Challenges and Solutions

Embarking on a real estate venture, especially one involving the transformative process of rewiring and wall removal, is a journey fraught with challenges and opportunities. In this chapter, we delve into the intricacies of these challenges, providing insight into the complexities of rewiring and wall removal while offering practical solutions to navigate these hurdles seamlessly.

The Transformative Power of Rewiring and Wall Removal

The decision to rewire and remove walls is often driven by a desire to create open, modern living spaces that align with contemporary design preferences. While these changes hold the potential to elevate a property's market value and appeal, they also introduce complexities that demand careful consideration and strategic planning.

Challenge 1: Electrical Rewiring Dilemmas

As the walls come down, so do the layers of complexity associated with electrical rewiring. Tackling outdated wiring, ensuring compliance with safety standards, and addressing unexpected issues that surface during the rewiring process pose significant challenges. The intricate network of electrical systems requires a nuanced understanding to ensure not only functionality but also safety and code adherence.

Solution 1: Professional Assessment and Planning

Engaging the expertise of licensed electricians is paramount when confronted with rewiring challenges. A professional assessment of the existing electrical infrastructure allows for the identification of potential issues and the formulation of a comprehensive rewiring plan. Collaborating with experienced electricians ensures that the rewiring process aligns with regulatory standards, mitigating risks and ensuring the safety of the property.

Challenge 2: Structural Implications of Wall Removal

The decision to remove walls brings about structural implications that extend beyond the aesthetic transformation. Load-bearing walls, though obstructive to an open layout, play a crucial role in supporting the integrity of a structure. Removing such walls requires a meticulous approach to maintain structural stability and prevent compromising the safety of the property.

Solution 2: Structural Engineering Expertise

Navigating the intricacies of wall removal demands the involvement of structural engineering expertise. Structural engineers possess the knowledge and skills necessary to assess load-bearing elements, determine the feasibility of wall removal, and prescribe solutions to maintain structural integrity. By collaborating with professionals in structural engineering, investors can confidently proceed with wall removal projects while safeguarding the property's stability.

Challenge 3: Unforeseen Complications and Budget Constraints

Real estate ventures are inherently unpredictable, and unforeseen complications often arise during the rewiring and wall removal phases. Whether encountering hidden structural issues, unforeseen wiring challenges, or budgetary constraints, investors must navigate these complexities with agility to ensure project success.

Solution 3: Contingency Planning and Flexibility

Contingency planning is a cornerstone of effective project management in real estate. Anticipating unforeseen complications and incorporating flexible timelines and budgets allow investors to adapt to evolving circumstances. Establishing contingency reserves and maintaining open communication with contractors enable investors to address challenges promptly, minimizing disruptions and ensuring the project stays on track.

Tackling rewiring and wall removal challenges in real estate ventures is a delicate dance of strategy, expertise, and adaptability. Recognizing the transformative power of these changes while navigating the complexities demands a holistic approach that prioritizes safety, compliance, and effective project management. By engaging professionals, leveraging structural engineering expertise, and implementing contingency measures, investors can orchestrate success amid challenges, transforming properties into modern, desirable homes that captivate the market and yield lucrative returns on investment.

Handling Big-Ticket Items with Finesse

In the intricate dance of real estate investment, confronting big-ticket items such as basements, foundations, and roofs demands a delicate touch and strategic finesse. This chapter explores the challenges posed by these significant components of a property and unveils nuanced approaches to navigate them with finesse, ensuring that real estate ventures not only withstand scrutiny but flourish in the competitive market.

The Weight of Big-Ticket Items: Defining Challenges

Basements, foundations, and roofs constitute the structural backbone of a property, influencing its longevity, stability, and market value. However, these components often introduce challenges that, if mishandled, can have profound implications on the success of a real estate venture.

Challenge 1: Basements: The Depths of Waterproofing and Transformation

Basements, while valuable for additional living space, present challenges related to waterproofing and transformation. Issues such as moisture infiltration, inadequate insulation, and the need for egress windows must be addressed to unlock the full potential of the basement and comply with safety standards.

Solution 1: Professional Waterproofing and Renovation

Engaging professionals specializing in basement waterproofing is pivotal for mitigating moisture-related challenges. Implementing effective drainage solutions, sealing foundation cracks, and ensuring proper insulation create a dry and habitable space. Collaborating with experienced contractors for basement renovation ensures that the transformed space aligns with modern design preferences while adhering to regulatory requirements.

Challenge 2: Foundations: Ensuring Structural Integrity

Foundations form the bedrock of a property's structural integrity, and issues such as settlement, cracks, or compromised stability demand immediate attention. Addressing foundation challenges is crucial to safeguarding the property's overall well-being.

Solution 2: Structural Assessment and Remediation

Conducting a comprehensive structural assessment, often with the expertise of structural engineers, allows for the identification of foundation issues and the formulation of remediation plans. This strategic approach ensures that the foundation is restored to optimal condition, preserving the property's stability and market desirability.

Challenge 3: Roofs: Guarding Against the Elements

Roofs, exposed to the elements, face challenges such as leaks, deterioration, and the need for periodic replacement. Tackling roofing issues requires a proactive stance to prevent water damage, ensure energy efficiency, and enhance the property's curb appeal.

Solution 3: Proactive Roof Maintenance and Replacement

Implementing a proactive roof maintenance plan, including regular inspections and timely repairs, is instrumental in preventing major issues. When replacement becomes necessary, opting for high-quality roofing materials and engaging experienced contractors ensures longevity and resilience against the elements.

Navigating Budgetary Considerations: The Art of Balance

Handling big-ticket items also necessitates navigating budgetary considerations, as addressing foundational or roofing challenges can be a substantial financial investment. Striking a balance between cost-effective solutions and long-term durability is an art that requires meticulous planning and informed decision-making.

In the grand symphony of real estate ventures, handling big-ticket items with finesse is an art that demands a blend of expertise, strategic planning, and a commitment to excellence. Investors who approach challenges related to basements, foundations, and roofs with a discerning eye and proactive mindset position their ventures for success. By prioritizing professional assessments, implementing strategic remediation measures, and balancing budgetary considerations, real estate ventures can not only weather the challenges posed by big-ticket items but also emerge as resilient, high-value properties in a competitive market.

The Flip Journey: From Demo to Design

Embarking on a house flipping journey is a thrilling endeavor that unfolds in stages, from the initial demolition to the meticulous design process. In this chapter, we'll take you on a guided walkthrough of a real flip project, unraveling the transformative journey that turns a dated property into a modern, market-ready home.

Stage 1: Demolition Drama

The flip journey kicks off with the dramatic phase of demolition. It's a moment of controlled chaos, where the echoes of sledgehammers and the resonance of power tools fill the air. In our real flip project, the walls came down to create an open concept living space, setting the stage for a design that aligns with contemporary preferences. While demo may seem like sheer destruction, it lays the foundation for the rejuvenation to come.

Stage 2: Rewiring and Infrastructural Overhaul

With the space cleared, the project delves into the crucial phase of rewiring and infrastructural overhaul. This is where the intricacies of electrical work, HVAC adjustments, and the elimination of outdated features take center stage. In our flip project, we faced the challenge of reconfiguring the electrical layout after removing walls. The solution involved professional assessment, meticulous planning, and a commitment to safety standards.

Stage 3: Design Dreams Unveiled

As the infrastructural elements fall into place, the flip journey transitions into the design phase—a juncture where creativity meets functionality. Our project embraced contemporary minimalism, featuring clean lines, neutral palettes, and an open layout. A focal point was the introduction of trendy design elements like open shelving, statement tiles, and matte black finishes. Each design choice was a deliberate step towards maximizing visual appeal and market desirability.

Stage 4: Kitchen and Dining Elegance

The heart of any home is its kitchen, and our flip project spared no effort in infusing elegance into this space. All-new white shaker cabinets, granite countertops, and a black granite sink created a harmonious blend of sophistication and functionality. The dining room received a makeover with new light fixtures and paneling, adding a touch of maturity to the overall design.

Stage 5: Masterful Bedrooms and Bathrooms

Venturing into the private domains, the flip project unfolded the design narrative in the bedrooms and bathrooms. The master bedroom showcased a floating countertop, shiplap walls, and luxurious black hardware. The ensuite bathroom became a spa-like retreat, featuring a barn door, dynamic color accents, and round mirrors—all curated for maximum market appeal.

Stage 6: Exterior Charm and Curb Appeal

The flip journey extended beyond the interiors to enhance the property's exterior charm and curb appeal. Landscaping efforts, a freshly painted garage door, and strategically chosen light fixtures elevated the property's visual impact. The goal was not just to create a stunning interior but to entice potential buyers from the moment they set eyes on the home.

Stage 7: Market Debut and Success

With the transformation complete, the flip project made its market debut, listing at a competitive price point. The property, located in the desirable Strongsville, Ohio, entered a market where Class A neighborhoods command attention. Multiple offers poured in within the first 24 hours, validating the meticulous planning, design choices, and market-savvy approach employed throughout the flip journey.

The walkthrough of this real flip project unravels the intricate tapestry of success woven through demolition, rewiring, and thoughtful design choices. Each stage of the journey contributes to the property's market readiness, ensuring it stands out in a competitive landscape. From demo to design, the flip journey is a testament to the art and science of real estate transformation, where vision, expertise, and attention to detail converge to create homes that captivate and command success in the market.

Milestones and Progress Updates

The house flipping odyssey is a dynamic venture marked by milestones and progress updates that serve as crucial markers on the path to success. In this chapter, we delve into the significance of tracking milestones, providing progress updates, and navigating the ever-evolving landscape of a real estate transformation.

Milestones: Guiding Lights in the Journey

Milestones in a house flipping project are akin to guiding lights, illuminating the progress made and charting the course ahead. These key markers not only signify accomplishments but also serve as motivational beacons for the entire team. Whether it's completing the demolition phase, achieving structural stability, or unveiling a stunning design element, each milestone propels the project forward.

Tracking milestones serves several purposes:

Progress Evaluation: Milestones offer a tangible way to evaluate progress. They allow investors, contractors, and stakeholders to assess whether the project is on schedule and meeting predetermined benchmarks.

Risk Mitigation: Identifying and celebrating milestones also aids in risk mitigation. By regularly assessing progress, potential challenges can be anticipated, allowing for proactive problem-solving before issues escalate.

Team Morale: Recognizing and celebrating milestones boosts team morale. It fosters a sense of accomplishment, instills confidence, and reinforces the collective effort invested in the project.

Decision-Making: Milestones serve as decision-making anchors. They provide a structured framework for assessing the project's trajectory, making informed decisions, and adjusting strategies when necessary.

Progress Updates: The Communication Lifeline

In the intricate tapestry of house flipping, effective communication is the lifeline that weaves together stakeholders, aligns expectations, and ensures everyone is on the same page. Regular progress updates play a pivotal role in this communication ecosystem.

Timely progress updates offer several advantages:

Transparency: Providing regular updates fosters transparency. It keeps all involved parties informed about the project's status, challenges encountered, and solutions implemented.

Client Confidence: For those working with external investors or clients, progress updates instill confidence. They demonstrate a commitment to transparency and a proactive approach to project management.

Issue Resolution: Progress updates serve as a platform to address challenges openly. By acknowledging issues and proposing solutions in real-time, potential roadblocks can be swiftly navigated.

Adaptability: In the dynamic landscape of real estate, adaptability is key. Progress updates facilitate agile decision-making, allowing the team to pivot strategies based on real-time insights.

Navigating the House Flipping Odyssey: A Case Study

Consider a scenario where a house flipping team sets a milestone to complete the structural renovations within a specified timeframe. Progress updates reveal that unexpected challenges in the foundation require additional attention. Transparent communication ensures that all stakeholders are aware of the situation, and a collaborative approach is taken to address the issue.

In this case, progress updates serve as a bridge between milestones, offering a real-time narrative of the project's evolution. The team navigates challenges with agility, adjusts timelines as needed, and ensures that the ultimate goal of a successful flip remains in focus.

In the ever-evolving dance of house flipping, milestones and progress updates are integral partners. They guide the journey, foster transparent communication, and contribute to the overall success of the venture. By acknowledging achievements, addressing challenges openly, and maintaining a flexible approach, investors can navigate the house flipping odyssey with finesse, turning each milestone into a stepping stone toward a profitable and market-ready property.

Competitive Pricing and Quick Sales

In the dynamic realm of house flipping, the art of setting the right price is a strategic maneuver that can be the difference between a property languishing on the market and a swift, lucrative sale. This chapter unravels the intricacies of competitive pricing, offering insights into the factors that influence it and the tactics to ensure a quick and successful sale.

Understanding the Market Dynamics

The process of setting the right price is a delicate dance with market dynamics. It involves a nuanced understanding of the local real estate landscape, recent comparable sales, and the unique features that distinguish the flipped property. In the world of house flipping, the price-performance nexus is a critical consideration.

Considerations for determining the right price include:

Comparable Sales (Comps): Analyzing recent sales of similar properties in the vicinity provides a benchmark for setting a competitive price. Comps offer insights into market trends, buyer expectations, and the perceived value of specific features.

Neighborhood Factors: The neighborhood itself plays a pivotal role in pricing. Factors such as school districts, amenities, and proximity to key locations influence buyer perceptions and, consequently, the property's value.

Property-Specific Enhancements: Any enhancements or unique features introduced during the flip should be carefully evaluated in the pricing strategy. From modern design elements to structural improvements, each adds value and contributes to the overall pricing equation.

Strategic Pricing Tactics: Balancing Profit and Market Appeal

While aiming for profitability is inherent in house flipping, strategic pricing involves a delicate balance between maximizing profit margins and ensuring market appeal. Several tactics contribute to this delicate equilibrium:

Competitive Analysis: Conducting a comprehensive analysis of competing properties in the market provides insights into the pricing landscape. This analysis helps identify opportunities for differentiation and positions the flipped property competitively.

Staging and Presentation: The visual presentation of the property, often achieved through professional staging, impacts its perceived value. Thoughtful presentation can justify a higher price point by showcasing the property's potential and lifestyle appeal.

Agile Pricing Adjustments: The real estate market is dynamic, and agility in pricing is a valuable asset. Monitoring market responses, gauging buyer feedback, and being willing to make strategic adjustments ensures the property remains attractive and competitive.

The Psychology of Pricing: Appealing to Buyer Perceptions

Understanding the psychology of pricing is an additional layer in the art of setting the right price. Price points carry psychological weight for buyers, influencing their perception of value and desirability. Considerations in this realm include:

Pricing Strategies: Tactics such as pricing just below a round number (e.g., $299,000 instead of $300,000) or emphasizing value-based pricing can trigger positive buyer responses.

Creating a Sense of Urgency: Strategic pricing can create a sense of urgency, prompting potential buyers to act swiftly to secure what appears to be a desirable property at a compelling price.

In the realm of house flipping, competitive pricing and quick sales are orchestrated like a symphony, with each note contributing to the overall harmony. Mastering the art of setting the right price involves a synthesis of market awareness, strategic pricing tactics, and an acute understanding of buyer psychology. By approaching pricing as a dynamic and strategic element of the house flipping process, investors can ensure their properties not only command attention in the market but also swiftly transition from listings to sold, maximizing both profitability and market impact.

Strategies for a Fast Sale: Accelerating the House Flipping Timeline

In the fast-paced world of house flipping, the ability to secure a swift sale is not just a measure of success but a testament to strategic acumen and market responsiveness. This chapter delves into proven strategies that accelerate the house flipping timeline, ensuring properties transition seamlessly from listing to sold, maximizing profitability and minimizing holding costs.

1. Mastering the Art of First Impressions: Curb Appeal Matters

The journey to a fast sale begins at the curb. Investing in curb appeal creates an immediate and lasting impression on potential buyers. From well-maintained landscaping to a fresh coat of exterior paint, attention to the property's exterior sets the stage for a positive walkthrough experience. The goal is to entice prospective buyers from the moment they lay eyes on the property, sparking their interest and curiosity.

2. Professional Staging: Elevating Visual Appeal

Professional staging is a game-changer in the realm of house flipping. By showcasing the property in its best light, staging creates an emotional connection for potential buyers. Thoughtfully arranged furniture, strategically placed decor, and a cohesive design aesthetic contribute to visual appeal. This not only makes the property more attractive in listing photos but also allows buyers to envision themselves living in the space, fostering a sense of connection that can expedite the decision-making process.

3. Pricing Strategically: Attracting Attention in a Competitive Market

Strategic pricing is a linchpin for a fast sale. Conducting a thorough analysis of comparable properties in the market helps in setting a competitive and appealing price point. Employing tactics such as pricing just below round numbers or emphasizing value-based pricing can capture buyer attention. Additionally, staying attuned to market dynamics and being agile in adjusting the price based on buyer feedback contributes to a dynamic pricing strategy that aligns with the goal of a swift sale.

4. Aggressive Marketing Campaigns: Visibility is Key

In a crowded real estate market, visibility is paramount. Implementing aggressive marketing campaigns across online and traditional channels ensures that the property reaches a broad audience. High-quality photos, compelling property descriptions, and targeted marketing efforts on real estate platforms and social media contribute to heightened visibility. Leveraging professional photography and creating engaging virtual tours further amplify the property's online presence, capturing the attention of potential buyers.

5. Hosting Open Houses: Creating a Buzz

Open houses remain a classic yet powerful strategy for generating interest and creating a sense of urgency. By allowing potential buyers to experience the property firsthand, open houses create a buzz and foster a competitive environment. Hosting these events strategically, perhaps on weekends or during peak real estate seasons, ensures maximum attendance. Additionally, coordinating with real estate agents to promote open houses can attract serious buyers actively seeking a property.

6. Flexibility in Negotiations: Streamlining the Closing Process

Flexibility in negotiations can significantly contribute to expediting the closing process. Being open to reasonable offers, addressing buyer concerns promptly, and demonstrating a collaborative approach fosters positive negotiations. A streamlined and efficient negotiation phase not only enhances the buyer's experience but also positions the property as an attractive and accessible investment.

7. Building Relationships with Experienced Real Estate Agents: Tapping into Networks

Establishing strong relationships with experienced real estate agents can be a strategic asset. Well-connected agents bring a network of potential buyers, market insights, and negotiation expertise to the table. Collaborating with reputable agents enhances the property's visibility and increases the likelihood of securing a fast and successful sale.

In the realm of house flipping, strategies for a fast sale are akin to orchestrating a symphony of success. From creating captivating first impressions to leveraging strategic pricing, each element plays a vital role in expediting the house flipping timeline. By adopting a comprehensive approach that encompasses visual appeal, marketing prowess, and collaborative negotiations, investors can ensure their properties not only stand out in the market but also transition seamlessly from listings to sold, unlocking the full potential of a successful house flipping venture.

Maximizing ROI: Secrets of Success

In the intricate game of house flipping, mastering the secrets to maximizing Return on Investment (ROI) is the key to a triumphant venture. This chapter unravels the strategies and insights that elevate the ROI game, with a particular focus on the transformative impact of opening spaces and incorporating creative designs.

The ROI Imperative: Balancing Investment and Returns

At the core of house flipping success lies the imperative to balance investments made in renovations, upgrades, and design enhancements with the anticipated returns. Maximizing ROI is not merely a financial goal; it is a strategic dance that requires astute decision-making, market awareness, and an acute understanding of buyer preferences.

Opening Spaces: A Strategic Paradigm Shift

One of the most impactful strategies for enhancing ROI is the strategic opening of spaces within a property. This goes beyond mere demolition; it involves a paradigm shift in the property's layout to create a sense of spaciousness and modernity. By removing non-structural walls, flipping projects can achieve a seamless flow, transforming cramped interiors into expansive, inviting spaces.

The benefits of opening spaces include:

Enhanced Perceived Value: Open floor plans are coveted by modern homebuyers. The removal of barriers between living spaces enhances the perceived value of the property, creating an environment that aligns with contemporary lifestyle preferences.

Improved Natural Light: Opening up spaces allows for better utilization of natural light. Well-lit interiors not only contribute to a positive living experience but also add to the overall aesthetic appeal of the property.

Adaptability: Open spaces offer adaptability, allowing potential buyers to envision personalized arrangements and uses for the expansive areas. This flexibility enhances the property's appeal to a diverse range of preferences.

Market Resonance: In the competitive real estate market, open spaces resonate with a broad spectrum of buyers. This increased market appeal can translate to a quicker sale and a higher return on the investment made in the property.

Creative Designs: Elevating Aesthetics and Value

While opening spaces lays the foundation for ROI optimization, creative designs act as the artistic brushstrokes that elevate a property to new heights. Implementing thoughtful and on-trend design elements not only enhances aesthetics but also contributes to the overall value proposition.

Strategies for incorporating creative designs include:

Accent Walls and Shiplap: Trendy design elements such as accent walls and shiplap can instantly transform a space, adding visual interest and a touch of sophistication. These features are relatively cost-effective yet yield high returns in terms of perceived value.

Modern Fixtures and Hardware: Upgrading fixtures and hardware to modern, sleek designs is a subtle yet impactful way to enhance a property's overall appeal. Black faucets, contemporary light fixtures, and stylish cabinet hardware contribute to a cohesive and appealing design narrative.

Innovative Kitchen and Bathroom Designs: Kitchens and bathrooms are focal points for many buyers. Innovative design choices, such as floating countertops, unique tiling, and modern cabinetry, elevate these spaces, leaving a lasting impression and contributing to a higher perceived value.

Functional and Stylish Storage Solutions: Incorporating creative storage solutions not only addresses practical needs but also adds an element of design innovation. Clever storage ideas enhance the property's functionality while showcasing a commitment to thoughtful design.

In the realm of house flipping, maximizing ROI is a harmonious blend of strategic spatial transformations and creative design flourishes. Opening spaces unlocks the potential for enhanced market appeal and quicker sales, while creative designs elevate aesthetics, leaving a lasting impression on potential buyers. By understanding the symbiotic relationship between space and style, house flippers can unveil the secrets of success in the ROI game, ensuring their ventures not only yield profitable returns but also stand out as exemplars of transformative and market-ready real estate.

Strategic Choices for Optimal Returns: Navigating the House Flipping Landscape

In the intricate world of house flipping, success hinges on a series of strategic choices that investors make throughout the process. This chapter delves into the key decisions and maneuvers that pave the way for optimal returns, guiding aspiring flippers through the nuanced landscape of real estate investment.

Understanding the House Flipping Landscape

House flipping is a dynamic and multifaceted journey that requires a comprehensive understanding of the real estate landscape. The strategic choices made by investors play a pivotal role in shaping the trajectory of the venture. From property acquisition to design decisions and pricing strategies, each choice is a calculated step towards achieving optimal returns.

1. Choosing the Right Property: The Foundation of Success

The journey towards optimal returns commences with the careful selection of the right property. Choosing a property with strong potential for value appreciation and market demand sets the foundation for a successful flip. Considerations in this phase include:

Location Analysis: Assessing the neighborhood, proximity to amenities, and market trends is crucial. Investing in up-and-coming neighborhoods or areas with growth potential can significantly impact future returns.

Condition Assessment: Evaluating the property's condition helps in estimating the required renovations and associated costs. Identifying properties with the potential for transformation while aligning with the target market is key.

Market Research: Conducting thorough market research provides insights into buyer preferences, pricing trends, and potential competition. This data informs decisions on property acquisition, ensuring alignment with market demands.

2. Financing Strategies: Balancing Risk and Reward

The financing strategy adopted for a house flip is a critical choice that influences overall returns. Balancing the need for upfront capital with the potential return on investment requires a nuanced approach. Key considerations in financing include:

Cash vs. Financing: Assessing the available capital and determining whether to use cash or secure financing impacts the initial investment and, consequently, the overall return. Factors such as interest rates and loan terms play a role in this decision.

Contingency Planning: Incorporating contingency funds into the financing plan is a strategic choice that guards against unforeseen expenses during the renovation process. Prudent financial planning minimizes risks and supports optimal returns.

3. Renovation and Design Decisions: Enhancing Value with Precision

The renovation and design phase is a crucible for strategic decision-making. Every choice, from the scope of renovations to design elements, contributes to the property's perceived value and market appeal. Strategic choices in this phase include:

Prioritizing Renovations: Identifying high-impact renovations that enhance the property's functionality and aesthetics is crucial. Strategic prioritization ensures resources are allocated where they yield the greatest returns.

Trend-Conscious Design: Incorporating design elements aligned with current trends enhances the property's visual appeal. Whether through modern fixtures, innovative layouts, or trendy finishes, staying attuned to design preferences maximizes market resonance.

Cost-Efficient Upgrades: Striking a balance between quality and cost is a strategic choice. Opting for cost-efficient upgrades that elevate the property's overall appeal without excessive expenditure contributes to optimal returns.

4. Pricing Strategies: Positioning for Success

Setting the right price is a strategic choice that significantly influences the speed of sale and overall returns. Leveraging competitive pricing strategies ensures the property remains attractive in the market. Key considerations include:

Market Analysis: Continuously analyzing market dynamics, comparable sales, and buyer behavior informs pricing decisions. Understanding the pulse of the market enables strategic positioning for optimal returns.

Agile Pricing Adjustments: The ability to make agile pricing adjustments based on market feedback and buyer response is a strategic advantage. Flexibility in pricing contributes to a faster sale and mitigates holding costs.

In the world of house flipping, optimal returns are woven into the tapestry of strategic choices made at every turn. From property selection and financing strategies to renovation decisions and pricing tactics, each choice contributes to the overall success of the venture. Navigating the house flipping landscape with strategic acumen and a forward-thinking approach empowers investors to not only unlock the full potential of their investments but also emerge as savvy navigators in the dynamic and rewarding realm of real estate.

Financing and Taxes Made Simple

As you delve into the dynamic world of house flipping, understanding the intricacies of financing and taxes becomes paramount. This chapter demystifies these complex aspects, offering straightforward insights and conservative underwriting strategies to empower house flippers on their financial journey.

Conservative Underwriting Strategies: A Pillar of Financial Stability

At the heart of successful house flipping lies the foundation of conservative underwriting. This strategic approach to financial planning ensures stability, mitigates risks, and positions investors for optimal returns. Implementing conservative underwriting strategies involves several key components:

Accurate Cost Projections: A conservative underwriting strategy begins with accurate cost projections. Thoroughly assessing the costs associated with property acquisition, renovations, holding expenses, and selling is foundational. Building a cushion for unforeseen expenses guards against financial surprises, fostering a resilient financial stance.

Realistic ARV Estimates: Anticipating the After Repair Value (ARV) of the property requires a realistic assessment. Conservative flippers resist the temptation to inflate ARV estimates, instead opting for a grounded evaluation based on comparable sales and market trends. Realistic ARV estimates contribute to more accurate financial planning and risk management.

Contingency Funds: Incorporating contingency funds into the budget is a prudent underwriting practice. Whether for unexpected renovation challenges, market fluctuations, or prolonged holding periods, contingency funds act as a financial safety net. This strategic allocation ensures financial resilience in the face of uncertainties.

Mindful Financing Structures: Choosing financing structures that align with conservative principles is pivotal. While leveraging external financing can amplify investment capacity, prudent flippers select options with favorable terms, reasonable interest rates, and manageable repayment schedules. Careful consideration of financing terms contributes to sustained financial health.

Sustainable Debt Management: Conservative underwriting extends to the management of debt. Flippers embrace a balanced approach to debt, ensuring that borrowed funds are invested strategically and do not overwhelm the financial structure. Sustainable debt management fosters financial stability and positions the investor for long-term success.

Financing Decisions: Balancing Risk and Reward

Navigating the financial landscape of house flipping involves making sound financing decisions that balance risk and reward. Whether utilizing personal funds, seeking loans, or exploring partnerships, the key is to align financing choices with the specific needs of each project. Some fundamental considerations include:

Cash vs. Financing: The choice between using personal cash reserves or securing external financing is a pivotal decision. Conservative flippers evaluate the opportunity cost of using cash, weighing it against potential returns, and consider financing options that optimize financial leverage.

Risk Assessment: Understanding the risks associated with different financing options is crucial. Conservative flippers conduct thorough risk assessments, considering factors such as interest rates, repayment terms, and potential market fluctuations. A clear understanding of risks informs decisions and safeguards financial stability.

Leveraging Partnerships: Strategic partnerships can be instrumental in financing house flipping ventures. Whether collaborating with private lenders, investors, or financial institutions, conservative flippers approach partnerships with a clear understanding of shared goals, expectations, and potential returns.

Taxes Made Simple: Navigating the Regulatory Landscape

Navigating the tax landscape is an integral aspect of house flipping, and simplicity is key. Understanding the tax implications of property acquisition, renovations, and sales ensures compliance while optimizing returns. Key considerations include:

Entity Structure: The choice of entity structure plays a significant role in tax planning. Conservative flippers often opt for structures like Limited Liability Companies (LLCs) or S Corporations, balancing liability protection with favorable tax treatment. Selecting the right entity structure is a strategic choice that impacts overall tax liability.

Capital Gains and Short-Term vs. Long-Term Taxation: House flipping ventures typically fall under short-term capital gains taxation. Conservative flippers are mindful of tax implications and plan accordingly. Understanding the tax brackets for short-term gains allows for effective tax planning and optimization of after-tax returns.

Deductions and Write-Offs: Maximizing deductions and eligible write-offs is a fundamental aspect of tax planning. Conservative flippers keep meticulous records of expenses related to property acquisition, renovations, and operational costs. Leveraging available deductions contributes to a reduction in taxable income.

Consulting Tax Professionals: Engaging tax professionals with expertise in real estate transactions is a strategic choice. Conservative flippers recognize the value of professional guidance in navigating the complexities of tax codes, ensuring compliance, and maximizing available deductions. Consulting tax professionals enhances financial efficiency and minimizes the risk of oversights.

In the realm of house flipping, mastering the financial landscape is a journey that demands strategic acumen and conservative underwriting. From accurate cost projections to thoughtful financing decisions and tax optimization, each choice contributes to financial mastery. By embracing conservative principles in underwriting and navigating financing and taxes with simplicity and foresight, house flippers can not only weather challenges but also position themselves for sustained success in the dynamic and rewarding world of real estate investment.

The S Corporation Advantage and Tax-Saving Tips

In the intricate realm of house flipping, maximizing financial efficiency is paramount. This chapter unravels the advantages of the S Corporation (S Corp) structure and offers invaluable tax-saving tips tailored for savvy house flippers. By strategically leveraging the benefits of an S Corp, flippers can optimize their tax position, enhance financial flexibility, and pave the way for sustained success in the dynamic world of real estate investment.

The S Corporation Advantage: Unveiling the Benefits

The S Corporation stands as a favored entity structure for many house flippers due to its unique advantages. Understanding these benefits is essential for flippers seeking to maximize tax efficiency and protect their financial interests:

Pass-Through Taxation: One of the hallmark advantages of the S Corp is its pass-through taxation feature. Unlike traditional corporations, S Corps do not pay federal income taxes at the entity level. Instead, profits and losses pass through to shareholders' individual tax returns. This pass-through structure can result in significant tax savings by avoiding double taxation.

Reduced Self-Employment Taxes: House flippers often generate income from both property sales and active involvement in the business. The S Corp structure allows for the distribution of profits as dividends, reducing the portion subject to self-employment taxes. This strategic distribution can result in substantial savings, especially for high-earning flippers.

Liability Protection: While providing tax advantages, the S Corp structure also offers limited liability protection to its shareholders. This shields personal assets from business liabilities, a crucial consideration in the inherently risk-laden landscape of real estate investment.

Flexibility in Income Distribution: S Corps provide flexibility in income distribution among shareholders. Flippers can strategically allocate income as salary and dividends, optimizing their tax position. This flexibility empowers flippers to tailor their compensation structure to align with their financial objectives.

Tax-Saving Tips for S Corporations: Navigating the Landscape

While the S Corporation structure presents distinct advantages, optimizing tax savings requires strategic planning and adherence to best practices. The following tips serve as a guide for house flippers aiming to extract the maximum benefit from their S Corp status:

Reasonable Compensation: Establishing a reasonable salary for active involvement in the business is crucial. The IRS scrutinizes S Corps that allocate minimal salaries to shareholders, aiming to classify excessive distributions as an attempt to avoid payroll taxes. Flippers should determine a fair and justifiable salary based on industry standards and the individual's contributions.

Documenting Business Expenses: Meticulous documentation of business expenses is a fundamental practice for S Corps. House flippers should maintain accurate records of all expenses related to property acquisition, renovations, operational costs, and other business activities. Comprehensive documentation not only supports tax deductions but also serves as a defense in case of audits.

Strategic Distribution Planning: Careful planning of income distributions is a key tax-saving strategy. By strategically balancing salary and dividend distributions, flippers can optimize their overall tax liability. Working closely with financial advisors to determine the most tax-efficient distribution strategy is a prudent practice.

Retaining Earnings for Growth: S Corps have the flexibility to retain earnings within the business for growth and reinvestment. While distributing profits is a common practice, flippers should evaluate the benefits of retaining earnings to fund future projects, capitalize on opportunities, and enhance overall financial resilience.

Regular Consultation with Tax Professionals: The tax landscape is dynamic, and regulations can undergo changes. Regular consultation with tax professionals ensures that flippers stay informed about evolving tax codes, take advantage of new opportunities, and remain compliant with existing regulations. Professional guidance contributes to strategic decision-making and optimal tax outcomes.

In the intricate dance of house flipping, the S Corporation emerges as a strategic player, offering a unique set of advantages and tax-saving opportunities. By harnessing the benefits of pass-through taxation, reducing self-employment taxes, and maintaining a flexible income distribution strategy, house flippers can position themselves for financial success. The S Corporation advantage, coupled with diligent adherence to tax-saving tips, becomes a powerful tool in the hands of savvy flippers seeking to navigate the complex financial landscape with finesse and foresight.

Building Your Real Estate Empire

Embarking on the journey of house flipping is not merely about individual deals; it's about cultivating a thriving real estate empire. This chapter unravels the snowball effect, illustrating how each successful flip contributes to the momentum that propels your venture from the first deal to sustainable business growth.

The First Deal: Igniting the Snowball Effect

Your inaugural house flip marks the inception of your real estate empire. As you navigate the intricacies of property acquisition, renovations, and successful sales, you lay the groundwork for future endeavors. The first deal is not just a transaction; it's a transformative experience that instills confidence, imparts practical knowledge, and sets the stage for what lies ahead.

Snowballing Success: The Dynamics of Growth

The snowball effect in real estate is a dynamic phenomenon where the success of one deal begets opportunities, relationships, and momentum for subsequent ventures. Here's how the snowball effect unfolds:

Business Relationships: Closing your first deal introduces you to a network of professionals – real estate agents, contractors, title companies, and more. These relationships, forged through the collaborative efforts of the initial flip, become integral to your future projects. Trusted connections enhance efficiency, streamline processes, and open doors to new opportunities.

Reputation and Credibility: A successfully executed first deal contributes significantly to your reputation and credibility within the real estate community. Positive word-of-mouth spreads, attracting potential partners, investors, and deals. As your reputation grows, so does the trust others place in your ability to deliver results.

Access to Financing: The successful closure of an initial deal enhances your financial profile, making you a more appealing candidate for financing. Lenders, recognizing your track record, become more inclined to offer favorable terms, thereby expanding your financial capacity for larger and more lucrative projects.

Market Insights: Every deal offers insights into market trends, buyer preferences, and potential pitfalls. These insights, gained through firsthand experience, empower you to make informed decisions and navigate market fluctuations with greater acumen. Each project becomes a lesson that contributes to your mastery of the real estate landscape.

Strategic Expansion: Scaling Your Real Estate Empire

Once the snowball starts rolling, strategic expansion becomes the next logical step. Scaling your real estate empire involves deliberate actions and calculated decisions:

Diversification: As your portfolio grows, consider diversifying your investments. Explore opportunities in different neighborhoods, property types, or even venture into complementary aspects of real estate, such as rental properties or commercial ventures. Diversification hedges risks and positions your empire for sustained growth.

Team Building: Scaling necessitates the formation of a robust team. As the volume of projects increases, assembling a competent team of professionals – project managers, contractors, real estate agents – becomes imperative. A well-coordinated team enhances efficiency, allowing you to take on multiple projects simultaneously.

Strategic Partnerships: Collaborating with strategic partners can catalyze growth. Forming partnerships with experienced investors, developers, or joint venture arrangements can provide access to larger deals and shared resources. Strategic partnerships amplify your capacity to take on ambitious projects.

Technology Integration: Embrace technology as a catalyst for efficiency. Implementing project management tools, leveraging data analytics for market research, and staying abreast of technological trends in real estate contribute to streamlined operations and informed decision-making.

The snowball effect, initiated by your first successful house flip, transforms your venture into a burgeoning real estate empire. Each deal, meticulously executed, contributes to the momentum that propels your business forward. With strategic expansion, diversification, and a keen eye on market dynamics, your empire becomes a dynamic force in the ever-evolving landscape of real estate investment. As the snowball gains momentum, the horizon is painted with the promise of a flourishing and enduring real estate empire.

Developing Key Relationships for Ongoing Success

In the dynamic realm of real estate ventures, the significance of cultivating key relationships cannot be overstated. This chapter delves into the pivotal role that strategic connections play in ensuring ongoing success and longevity in the competitive landscape of property investment.

Building a Robust Network: The Foundation of Success

At the heart of ongoing success in real estate lies a robust network of relationships that extend beyond mere transactions. Whether you are a seasoned investor or just starting, fostering connections with various stakeholders is akin to fortifying the foundation of your real estate endeavors. The key relationships that contribute to ongoing success encompass a diverse array of professionals and entities.

1. Real Estate Agents: Navigating the Market with Expertise

Establishing solid ties with experienced real estate agents is a strategic move that enhances your market insights and access to valuable opportunities. A skilled agent not only aids in property acquisitions but also serves as a conduit to market trends, potential deals, and crucial information that can impact your investment decisions. Cultivating a symbiotic relationship with real estate agents fosters a collaborative approach to identifying and capitalizing on lucrative ventures.

2. Contractors and Builders: Reliable Partners in Project Execution

In the intricate process of flipping houses, the relationships you forge with contractors and builders are instrumental. These professionals form the backbone of successful project execution. Trustworthy contractors contribute not only to the quality of renovations but also to adherence to timelines and budgets. Nurturing these relationships ensures a reliable and efficient team, essential for the seamless progression of your real estate ventures.

3. Financial Institutions: Securing Solid Financing Partnerships

Access to capital is a cornerstone of ongoing success in real estate. Developing strong ties with financial institutions, private lenders, or investors can open avenues for favorable financing terms, increased borrowing capacity, and expedited approval processes. Building a reputation as a reliable borrower enhances your ability to secure financing for both modest and ambitious projects, fostering sustained growth.

4. Title Companies: Ensuring Smooth Transactions

The importance of a proficient title company cannot be overstated in real estate transactions. Collaborating with reputable title companies ensures the legality and smooth transfer of property ownership. Establishing ongoing relationships with these entities streamlines the closing process, mitigates potential legal issues, and enhances the overall efficiency of your investment transactions.

5. Local Authorities and Planning Departments: Navigating Regulatory Waters

Successful real estate ventures necessitate compliance with local regulations and zoning laws. Cultivating relationships with local authorities and planning departments facilitates a smoother navigation of regulatory waters. Proactive engagement with these entities not only ensures adherence to legal requirements but also positions you as a responsible and informed investor within the community.

6. Networking with Peers: Learning and Growing Together

Participating in real estate networking events, forums, and groups provides opportunities to connect with peers, share experiences, and glean insights from seasoned investors. These relationships contribute to ongoing learning, offer a platform for idea exchange, and foster a supportive community that can prove invaluable during challenges or market fluctuations.

7. Real Estate Attorneys: Safeguarding Legal Interests

In the intricate landscape of real estate, legal nuances are inevitable. Establishing relationships with proficient real estate attorneys is essential for safeguarding your legal interests. From contract reviews to navigating complex legal scenarios, a trusted attorney becomes a valuable asset in protecting your investments and ensuring legal compliance.

Cultivating Long-Term Partnerships: The Art of Relationship Management

Beyond the initial establishment of relationships, the art of ongoing success lies in cultivating and maintaining long-term partnerships. Regular communication, reciprocation of value, and ethical conduct contribute to the sustainability of these connections. The ongoing success of your real estate ventures hinges on the strength and continuity of the key relationships you cultivate, creating a resilient network that withstands the tests of time and market dynamics.

In the ever-evolving landscape of real estate ventures, the enduring power of strategic connections becomes the linchpin for ongoing success. From real estate agents and contractors to financial institutions and legal professionals, each key relationship contributes to the robustness of your investment endeavors. As you navigate the intricacies of the real estate market, the cultivation of these relationships becomes not just a strategic choice but a cornerstone for building a lasting legacy in the dynamic world of property investment.

CONCLUSION

In the journey through this comprehensive guide to house flipping, we've delved into the intricacies of transforming real estate ventures into a thriving empire. From the foundational principles of the 70% rule to the art of strategic relationship building, each chapter unraveled critical facets of the house flipping process. The power of taking action emerged as a guiding principle, propelling aspiring investors to dive into the market with confidence and determination.

Navigating the real estate market, leveraging the MLS, and decoding the 70% rule became not just theoretical concepts but actionable strategies for success. The chapters on creative design, tackling big-ticket items, and handling challenges equipped readers with the knowledge and insights to turn potential obstacles into opportunities.

The real essence of this guide lies in its practicality. It goes beyond theory, offering a step-by-step walkthrough of a real flip project. The emphasis on open spaces, trendy design elements, and maximizing ROI through strategic choices became the signature of a winning formula. Each chapter unfolded as a lesson, combining theory with real-world applications, preparing readers for the dynamic landscape of house flipping.

As the journey progressed, the concept of the snowball effect became the overarching theme, illustrating how each successful flip contributes to the momentum that propels an individual from a novice investor to a seasoned entrepreneur. Strategic relationships emerged as the cornerstone of ongoing success, emphasizing the collaborative nature of the real estate industry.

In essence, this guide is a blueprint for transforming aspirations into accomplishments. It is not just a book; it's a mentor, guiding readers through the complexities of real estate ventures, offering insights garnered from experience, and laying the foundation for building a lasting empire.